LET'S TRANSFORM TOGETHER

A JOURNEY OF BROKEN HEARTS TO MENDED HEARTS

UNNATI JHAVERI

Contents

Preface

This book is for all the people who are in relationships and for individuals who would like to be in a relationship. All the topics in this book have been spoken about in great detail by others before me. This is just my version of it. This book will help you to understand your part in any relationship rather than taking the route of blaming others. It will help you to look within and identify your own patterns, which may not be serving you anymore, and how you can reinvent the wheel for yourself. It will help you to become more emotionally independent and understand the true meaning of companionship.

Relationships are a blessing for our growth as individuals when we see it in that light. The topics will help you to change your perspective towards relationships and take an approach which has a higher purpose, and which is not related to surface level happiness. It will help you to think of your family of origin and the behaviours that come from your upbringing, and whether those are still in alignment with you or need to be changed in some ways as you grow and mature. This book also talks about the aspects that will enhance your relationship and how to integrate those internally, which will lead to a more trusted and fulfilling relationship. I sincerely hope you enjoy this book, and it helps you to break certain patterns but also helps you to have a better relationship with your own self and your partner.

Acknowledgements

I would like to take this opportunity to thank every person that has been a part of my life. Some people have always been there, and some have come and left at the right time for me to grow. I am extremely grateful for my parents, family, friends, teachers, and guides who have all been an extremely integral part of my life and have supported me tremendously. The person I am today is through all my experiences and lessons I have learnt and will continue to learn. There are a lot of people that have inspired me, those who believe in themselves irrespective of their backgrounds, and who in their hearts know what they want to do with their lives and are ready to achieve it, by walking on the right path. I have come across several people like this and their sheer being has inspired me in ways I cannot express. I may not even know all these people personally, but their stories and determination have taught me a lot. I call these people true warriors of lives who have come in my life at the right time to inspire me and push me out of my comfort zone. These experiences and lessons have been etched on my soul and will always be with me. I bow down to each person who has been a part of my life in some way with utmost humility and gratitude. Thank you.

Diving Deep Into your Core Self

CHAPTER ONE

Competitiveness

Vikram and Sarah were struggling in their relationship. They were both doing very well in their individual careers but were feeling a huge disconnect from each other. For Vikram, he was craving time from Sarah. Sarah's work was extremely demanding but had also become a priority for her. On the surface, they were an ideal couple, as their friends and family looked up to them in many ways. Everyone from the outside felt they had a perfect marriage but that was far from the reality.

Vikram and Sarah, once high school sweethearts, had a long-distance relationship during their courtship period. As soon as they got married, they became so preoccupied with their family and individual careers that they could not spare time for their relationship. They took each other for granted to a large extent. Communication between them started lagging, and their relationship was never a priority. Through the years the distance kept growing till they realised and recognized it. Over time, they grew further apart, and the strain fell harder on the relationship which was once nurturing and blossoming. They were unable to understand each other which brought in a lot of criticism and unwanted blame towards each other. They were unable to communicate beyond a point as the anger and disappointment had seeped into the delicate crevices of life. As years passed the bitterness escalated. The relationship spiralled and became a YOU vs ME situation instead of US. Slowly competitiveness crept into their bond in each area- from an emotional, financial, and mental perspective. They were not representing the same team anymore.

This is indeed a turning point where one needs to understand and seek professional help as it then takes uglier and more unbearable turns. Competitiveness in a relationship has the potential to cause a complete shutdown for individuals.

They both decided to come for counselling to further understand how to care for the wilted flower that their relationship had become. After understanding their background and childhood what surfaced was, that they were carrying hurt and pain from before into their relationship. It reflected in their partnership as parts of each that were not healed from their past.

When we do not heal from our past, it carries forward into all existing relationships, thus expecting the other to make us feel better. But is that a correct expectation to have from any relationship? Or is it our sole responsibility to work on our own healing?

Vikram and Sarah were both happy for each other regarding their work but were unable to participate in each other's celebratory moments. Vikram was doing better financially and if he offered anything to Sarah materialistically, she would right away reject it saying she did not need any of this. She was dismissing Vikram's sentiment through her action because Sarah did not feel understood by Vikram. Sarah was not looking for any materialistic things but rather more meaningful gestures which Vikram was unable to understand. Due to not spending enough time with each other and not prioritizing the relationship through the years, they had not understood that there love languages had changed over time. Therefore, they had a lot to catch up on and learn about each other.

When a superiority or inferiority complex sets in a relationship, it becomes challenging to find empathy for each other. This was never a part of the relationship but rather what Vikram and Sarah felt all along their life and never healed from. They both came from very humble backgrounds and proving themselves at every juncture was extremely important. They both felt a deep sense of inadequacy while growing up which they had never come around and worked through. Through therapy, they were able to understand what the hindrance was and how to work through it. It starts first by working on yourself. Over time, they learned how to communicate, understand, and respond to each other's needs.

Competitiveness sprouts from the core feeling of inadequacy. When one does not feel enough in any situation or relationship, one tends to carry it forward almost always. This dimension creates a constant need to prove oneself, over and over again. Therefore, it can sometimes become difficult to see your own loved ones flourish. It does not make anyone bad, but it is a cue for individuals to look within and heal. Individuals who come from humble backgrounds have grown up seeing their parents struggle and thus it becomes imperative for them to want a good life. This can lead to an incessant need to prove oneself. It does not work in a relationship where one is trying to become better than the other, because intimate relationships are not a ground for competitiveness but rather togetherness.

For most individuals, the feeling of inadequacy may have been projected by another in a situation or in a series of situations which then becomes an inner dialogue. Essentially it is a mere borrowed belief the individual has taken on themselves and what the individual thinks of themselves which is temporary as it is not the individual's core personality. When we are young, we do not have an adult brain to analyse, and we tend to believe what our surroundings show us. But as we become adults, we develop an analytical mind, more in touch with the reality of life and we see that this thought pattern needs to change. Unfortunately, we do not pay heed to this core of competitiveness, we do not heal ourselves and it makes its way into every relationship that we co-create.

Every individual is here to learn and improve themself through life experiences and teachings. Feeling adequate, predominantly is a spiritual journey that we need to work through by first, getting to know ourselves. Understanding self and connecting to a higher power is the answer to feeling adequate. When we understand the work of the creator, we do not feel the burden of inadequacy. We will look at ourselves as beings who have come here to learn and grow and that can change our entire perspective shedding the inadequacy belief and moving towards being whole.

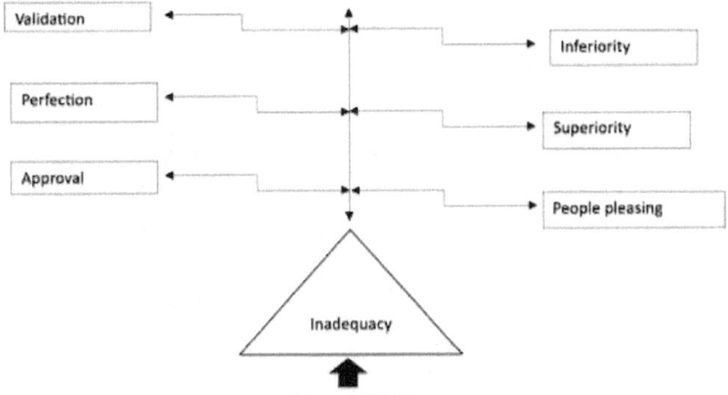

(Beliefs that have been passed from the environment, society, and others)

Illustration: Competitiveness

CHAPTER TWO

Victimization

Arun & Jyoti were going through a rough patch in their marriage due to living in a joint family. Arun felt sandwiched in this situation and over time started feeling very disconnected from Jyoti. He felt that no matter what he was trying to do for her it was never enough. Before they got married, they both had decided they would move into their own home but with time Arun's parents' health deteriorated and being the only son, he had to make a change in their plans of living separately. He knew it was not fair for Jyoti, but he felt very stuck in this situation. Even after all this, Arun decided if any condo would come up in the same building, he would make sure to shift there but it was not something that happened in the last 10 years. Simultaneously, Jyoti had lost all patience during this period and had started feeling a disconnect from Arun as well. Slowly, as time passed, the distance between Arun and Jyoti kept growing. They would argue over everything when that was not how the relationship had started. They were still absolutely in love with each other. But it was buried under layers of mistrust, anger, disappointment, and sadness, due to which they were unable to reach and express the love they had for each other.

With time, it was getting too much for Jyoti, so she started talking about their situation to all her friends which made Arun look bad and in return she was gaining sympathy by becoming a victim in the situation. She would constantly feel sad for herself and question her choices largely in her mind.

What she was asking for was not wrong but sometimes in life, we forget to pair what we want with patience and trust. It was not that Arun was not agreeing but given the circumstances, the development was not in their favour.

Jyoti felt not being understood by Arun and vice-versa. Slowly things were going out of hand, and they were constantly arguing and fighting as all the suppressed emotions were taking over. At some point, they decided to look out for professional help as they were unable to solve the matter between them.

Jyoti came from a background where she was in a very privileged position and Arun also came from a well-to-do family. For Jyoti, it was very easy to get what she wanted, and, in her childhood, she had not had a situation that did not go according to her wish. Stepping into this marriage with Arun and her love for him made him convince her to wait for a bit after which they could live separately. Jyoti had lost all patience, and it was very difficult for Jyoti to accept her situation after 10 years of being married.

The feeling of victimisation has its roots in feeling a sense of lack of control. When an individual feels they are losing control which by itself is not easy for anyone, as we are not okay with uncertainty, we will go to any lengths to keep that control even at our own cost, as uncertainty comes with its fears. Jyoti had always felt a sense of control and when she did not feel it, she wanted to get back the control in some way, and she felt unconsciously becoming a victim would help. But it was that exact action that was creating more distance between her and Arun. The lack of control made Jyoti feel unimportant. It resulted in her feeling more and more distant from her husband.

Arun was feeling a huge sense of loss and inadequacy. On one hand he was feeling guilty for not keeping up to his promise but on the other hand not being able to understand Jyoti and her behaviours. All their common friends now knew what was going on in their marriage and he felt extremely disappointment in himself.

Being the only son, Arun felt a great deal of responsibility towards his ageing parents. Throughout his childhood, Arun felt a sense of loss as at a very young age he lost his sibling in a tragic accident of drowning. With this situation, his parents looked up to Arun and all their expectations rested on Arun's shoulders. For Arun, it was not easy as he had taken both his and his deceased brothers load on himself. Arun would always doubt his abilities and feel he was not doing enough for his parents, despite his parents never making him feel that way. This was something he had taken on himself as a child especially after losing his sibling.

For both, their past feelings had surfaced back again which were playing a huge role in the distance caused in their relationship. Jyoti's behaviours were pressing on the feeling of inadequacy for Arun and Arun was pressing on the feeling of being unimportant for Jyoti.

While taking therapy they were able to understand their own patterns and the seeds sown from their patterns which had been left unhealed and were causing the distance in their relationship. Through time they understood their own needs and each other's needs to be able to have a more stable relationship. They slowly worked through healing those patterns and changing their perspective which helped them. Most importantly, they were able to accept each other and their reality which made all the difference to their equation. They recognized it was not something they were doing to get back to each other in any way, but they were both feeling lost in their own life which made them say and do things they would otherwise never do. They strengthened their relationship with themselves, and they were able to feel important and adequate from within rather than expecting their partner to make them feel that way. This change in perspective was a game-changer. They understood and built a better relationship with themselves. In an intimate relationship having 20% expectations is alright but for the remaining 80% an individual needs to work and generate the feeling from within.

Accepting one's life for what it is, is a spiritual journey. We all come with a set of expectations based on our own needs, but it is important to understand that we may know what we need but we don't understand the correct time for the same. This is something we need to surrender to the higher power who can step in and take control of the situation and our needs. We need to trust that there is a higher power who is looking after us and knows what we need at the right time. This understanding comes only when we look inward rather than outward for solutions. After another two years, Arun and Jyoti were able to move into their own home in the same building, and with time Jyoti's relationship with Arun's parents also got better.

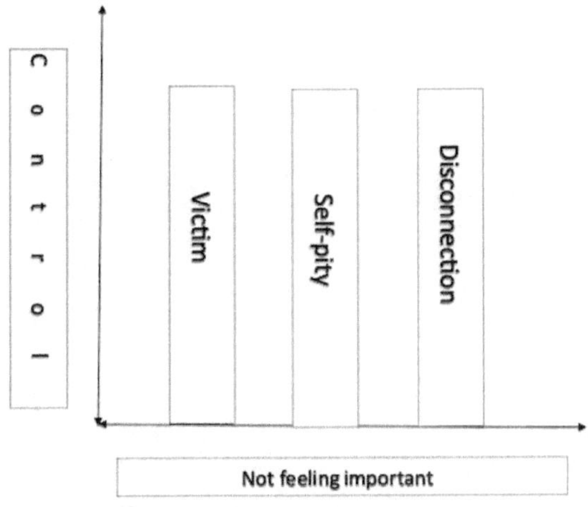

The above illustration shows the direct proportion: the more one feels less important;
the more one wants to control.

Illustration: Victimisation

CHAPTER THREE

Blame Game

Raj and Kavita were stuck in a cycle of constant blame.

They were introduced to each other through common friends and had a beautiful courtship period. They understood each other as they both came from very difficult backgrounds where Raj went through a lot of beating because he was extremely naughty as a child. Kavita, on the other hand, was the middle child so would often get blamed for things she did not do. They both felt a deep sense of rejection which made them feel they did not matter. But when they met each other, they noticed a sense of fulfilment as they understood and accepted each other irrespective of their past and how they were treated. (Please know we are not here to blame anyone, but there is an impact on how everyone is treated, and we need to work through those pieces to heal).

They both were absolutely in love and happy with each other. Their relationship sailed through smoothly for the first few years of marriage. They had two gorgeous children a few years down the road.

Soon enough after they had children, the relationship started shifting. They both were working professionals and with added responsibilities, they were not able to give their relationship time, which they knew and understood. But more importantly, they were sensing a loss because, over the years they had built many expectations from each other which were not getting fulfilled anymore. They would have constant fights and arguments and were unable to understand what changed so drastically. They wondered how they reached this point of utter frustration and unhappiness in their relationship. They would constantly blame each other for how they individually felt. They would use bitter language to purposely hurt each other. It would happen in front of their children who then started taking sides. Raj and Kavita saw this as a red flag and an unhealthy environment at home which was far from what they wanted it to be.

When they came in for therapy, they were at a stage of feeling completely disconnected and disappointed with each other. Through the sessions, they understood the similar wounds from the past. Their wound was a deep sense of rejection which led them to feel as if they did not matter, and the unwantedness was resurfacing back for them.

The reason this happens is we believe that when we are in love, it takes away all the pain from the past. Sadly, it is only temporary. When things fizzle down, the unhealed wound from the past surfaces back up as we are meant to heal it. It is a way for our body, mind and soul to nudge us to give attention to what needs to be healed. Childhood wounds will spring back up until there is a perspective shift and are worked upon seriously.

Both Raj and Kavita had to work through their past and reach a place where they were able to forgive themselves for carrying this feeling forward that they did not matter. They had to change their perspective towards others and become more understanding of their experiences. They had to let go of the past and live in their present. Most importantly they needed to understand their self-worth and how much they matter to themselves. They had to build a relationship with themselves to understand their internals, which they had never done. They needed to understand their own value, so they were not dependent on others to dictate their value. They had to stop being dependent on each other to make them feel as if they mattered, but rather generate that feeling of they mattered from within. Yes, in a relationship it is okay to depend a little on each other but not totally as Raj and Kavita did. They finally were able to take their reigns into their own hands which changed their equation. Slowly they were able to see each other for who they had become and re-adjusted their basic expectations to take into consideration the other person's needs and capacity. They were in a better place after they had worked on their past wounds, which over time reduced the distance and disappointment they felt towards each other.

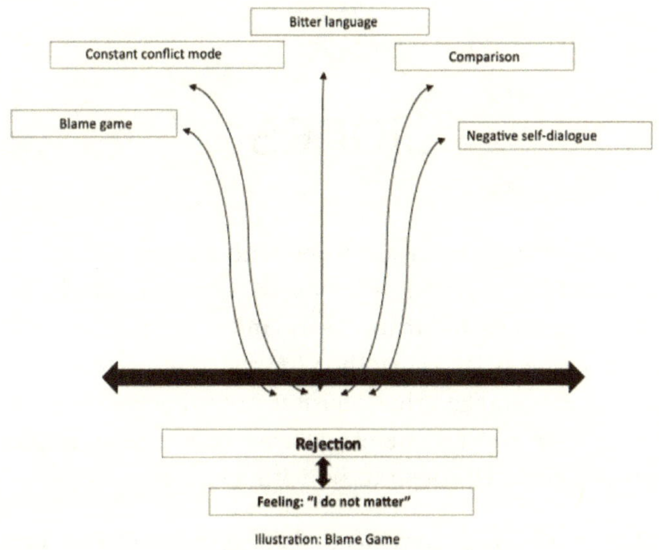

Illustration: Blame Game

CHAPTER FOUR

Clones

Rajiv and Priya were meant to be with each other, which was something everyone who knew them felt. They had been best friends for many years and one fine day they decided to be with each other for the rest of their life. They did contemplate this decision from time to time but felt they each had no one else. Please take time to reflect if this is a reason enough to be with someone.

Over time, they convinced themselves and everyone around them was convinced as well. Rajiv and Priya got married and moved to London as they both wanted to explore a place away from home and they both were offered good job opportunities. They had a fluctuating relationship where they had good and not-so-good days. One of the most difficult situations for them both was the differences in their opinions. They would always think to themselves that before marriage they used to align much more than after which they were not able to comprehend and come to terms with.

Two years into their marriage the love was slowly getting replaced by fights and arguments. They were surprised with what was going on as they would never be able to understand each other's needs which led to more distance and more sadness. One of their friends recommended therapy. Both were extremely hesitant as this was not something they had even remotely thought of. It was a process for them to convince themselves which took another year, where things went from bad to worse between them.

Rajiv & Priya came from families who had been through a very difficult time and had made a name in society through a lot of hard work over the years. Their societal image was extremely important to them, irrespective of what they felt or sensed. Feelings and emotions were not something that came very easily to them. They did not speak or express as freely. It was more about keeping up with a certain image they had created in the society. This was a part of how they both had been brought up. Please know that we are not here to blame anyone for any kind of behaviour but they all impact humans in ways we cannot understand, therefore it is important to heal from these impacts. For each of their families, it was only one way of living, which was safeguarding their societal image. Nothing less was imaginable or acceptable. To keep this image of always being good and put together, also led to the need to always be right turning it into my way or the highway eventually. This caused a lot of burden and expectations for everyone who was a part of their family.

The need to be right can often stem from a lack of trust. It is hard for individuals to trust others, if and whether they will be accepted, when they are not right therefore keeping up to a certain image becomes imperative.

Both Rajiv and Priya were very set in their ways which worked in their favour when they were friends, but once they started living together, things changed. Through unpacking in therapy, they understood their level of expectations from each other which when they were unable to deliver would lead to a fight because it was important for each of them to fight for being right. Over time they were stuck in the same cycle, which led them to lose themselves in all the chaos. They both were trying to change each other to fit a mould that they had made in their own minds. But is this possible? Can we change someone to fit the mould we create for them?

It was difficult for both Rajiv and Priya to accept what they each brought into the relationship. Instead, they were obsessed with creating clones of themselves through each other which was an unlikely event. We cannot control or change someone to become like us. Yes, we all know this but when it comes to an intimate relationship, we have such high expectations from our partners to behave, think, talk, and feel, just the way we want them to feel. This causes humongous disappointment.

Then the question arises, is it okay to have any expectations from our partners?

Yes, it is okay to have expectations from our partner, but they must be in alignment with the opposite person's capacity or else it will cause more distance. For this, each person needs to understand their partner. From a percentage point of view, it is okay to have 15%-20% expectations from our partner but 80% is our own work, where we need to depend on ourselves for our own happiness and how we feel.

For Rajiv & Priya, they needed to lower their expectations and understand their own need to want the other person to be just like them. This behaviour stemmed from the fear of feeling a lack of control, which came from a place of lack of trust. When we are unable to trust others, it becomes very important for them to be like us so that we feel safe when we see and feel the familiarity. When we see any differences, it becomes extremely difficult for us to accept as it invokes the fear of lack of control which sends the signal of mistrust.

For Rajiv & Priya, it took time, but they needed to work on trusting themselves and extending that trust to each other and everyone else around them. They also had to learn to trust the process of life and to be able to not live in non-acceptance. While working on this they had to understand their ancestry and the circumstances they had gone through which caused the lack of trust which was ingrained in their family system. They needed to open and understand those relationships and what landed on each of them and how it played out in their life. They had to do intergenerational work and change perspectives and make shifts by really looking within and by taking on a compassionate lens towards self, each other, and everyone around them.

Many emotions came up for them but through time and understanding, they both were in a better place where it was not only about what they wanted but they considered each other's needs as well. They both walked beautifully on the road of acceptance where they saw and tackled the differences that came with each of them and celebrated them. Over time, the need to be right and the idea of my way or the highway melted away helping them to grow their trust in self and each other and letting go of the need to control another.

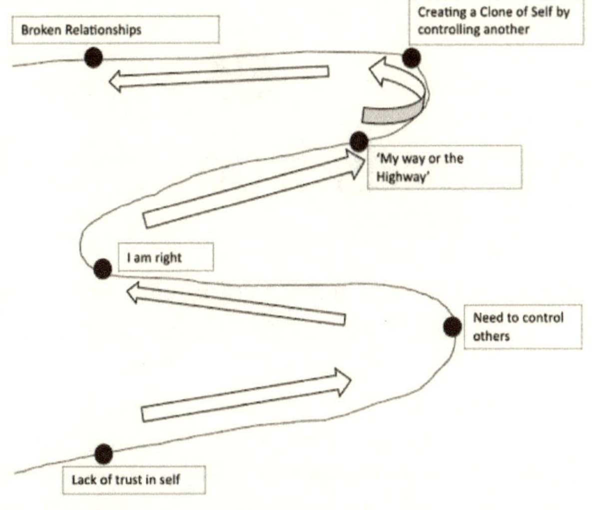

Illustration: Clones

CHAPTER FIVE

Wounds from the Past

Manav and Aashna had a very intense relationship. They were introduced at a friend's party and connected the very first time they met. For them, it felt like they had known each other for many years during their very first-time meeting. They started getting to know each other and soon enough felt a sense of comfort with each other. They soon started dating and their relationship intensified. They would feel a very strange pull towards each other constantly. Neither of them understood this magnetic pull. They had dated other people before but never felt this sense of connection. They felt like they must have known each other for many lifetimes.

The more intense their relationship was, the more extremes they felt. Be it fights and arguments or the rush of emotions- it all ranged to the extremes. The balance was missing in this relationship.

They both came from very hard-working backgrounds; both were professionals and did well for themselves. They were both spiritually inclined and would often think about how they came so close in such a short period. Within three months of knowing each other, they were married.

They moved into their own home and soon enough the disagreements escalated. They would have intense fights which they managed well during their courtship period but now, either one of them would storm out and would not communicate with each other for days together. This became a pattern between them over time. The core reason for all their fights was when they felt they lacked enough attention from each other. When it came to getting attention, all understanding was lost for both. They would crave for each other during periods of distance, but their ego did not allow them to bend. As time passed, this became a comfortable cycle for them both, leading to toxic behaviour. This went on for six years and one fine day they both realised this was not working for them anymore. They were unable to comprehend how to step out of this vicious cycle.

Manav and Aashna decided to give it one last go and started therapy. They wanted to work towards bridging the gap between them but always ended up fighting and arguing in the sessions. Either of them would say something that would trigger the other person. Many times, knowingly they would say things to hurt the other person as they were so angry with each other. Through multiple sessions, they understood they were not only angry with each other but themselves as well. This understanding was a huge turning point. Through further unpacking they both revealed that they both had a past which they did not share due to the fear of rejection and a lingering feeling of shame.

It was indeed a rocky road, but they eventually reached a place where they were able to share that they both had been subjected to sexual abuse as children. This information weighed heavily on both. They would blame themselves and this trauma made them feel empty about themselves internally. When they would fight and argue, it would take them back to feeling unsafe as they did in childhood. This was the core reason for the high intensity between them. They would feel safe when they got attention mutually. So much so that it was essential for them to survive. They both in their way felt very unsafe in the world but it was only with each other that they felt secure. Therefore, when they fought, they did not understand what they would do or how to mend it.

Manav and Aashna as individuals had to work on themselves to learn how to feel safe and work through the trauma they had been through. Depending on each other to a broad extent was unhealthy and surely was not helping as they did not know how to help the opposite person. Therefore, attending to themselves first and doing their individual work was very important. They understood that they both felt very unsafe when either of them would storm out or reject the opposite person by not talking and looking at them. It took them back to their childhood, when they felt unheard and unseen. This was very familiar to their trauma as nobody heard them after saying "no" multiple times. It would bring up similar past emotions which would turn into such high intensity. When Manav and Aashna were able to share their trauma, they felt a renewed sense of compatibility, not rejection in the moment but rather support. They felt like a big burden was released from them.

The physical intimacy between them was steady for the first three years. But as the distances and their past trauma resurfaced, the intimacy diminished slowly. When healing is not given enough priority, the trauma keeps surfacing till one pays heed to it. It is a way for our body to communicate, and to pay attention to where healing is required. Very often we tend to compartmentalise and do not do anything about it thinking it will get better in time. But trauma is something that needs to be worked on, it does not just go away. When any individual is put through a situation where their freedom is violated, it scars the person and working through the trauma is like putting balm on our wounds from the past.

With time passing, both Manav and Aashna were able to understand their own needs and their partner's needs and how to show up in the relationship. They were able to understand the importance of feeling safe within themselves and with each other. Over time their intimacy got better, and they were able to support each other through it. They felt re-connected with themselves which also made them feel re-connected to each other. They stopped blaming themselves for their trauma. They took a spiritual approach where they were able to work through each phase of life and grow as individuals through that process.

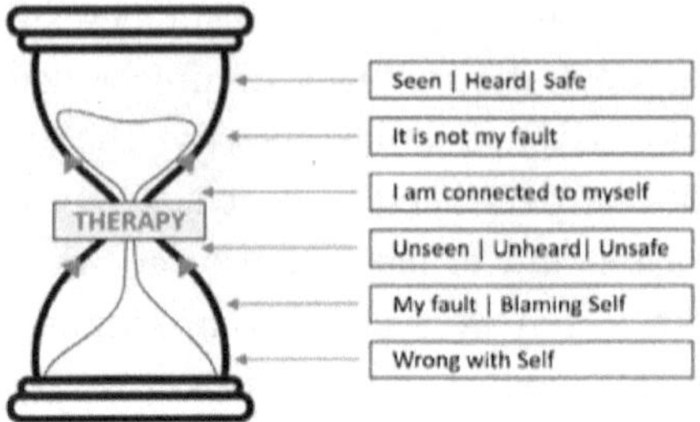

Illustration: Wounds from the Past

CHAPTER SIX

Physical Intimacy

Arundhati came from a very abusive family where she experienced an environment of chaos. She used to walk on eggshells around adults which led her to miss her childhood and become an adult very early on. Arundhati and her younger sister were instilled with fear. She had grown up watching men disrespect women, physically abuse them and bring other women to their home. She never had many friends while growing up except one close friend. Arundhati was always an introvert and would not speak much.

In university, she met Armaan who was a very kind and considerate person. Through time they became good friends which eventually led them to have feelings for each other. Armaan came from a very broad-minded, modern and emotionally available family. He would always show up for Arundhati and especially after understanding her childhood history he would try his best to support her and care for her.

Things were fine between them but somewhere due to Arundhati's past, it was not easy for her to trust Armaan 100% even though she truly wanted to express love and care to him as she genuinely loved him. That was a point of extreme difficulty in their relationship which started becoming more visible once they got married. Physical intimacy became harder between the two of them as it was hard for Arundhati to give herself to him completely. It felt very disconnected for them both. As time passed, the distance between them grew. During the first six months after their marriage, their physical intimacy suffered greatly. Armaan would bring this topic as a discussion and Arundhati would cave inward and would shut down completely. She would not speak a word which was very surprising to Armaan. They both loved each other immensely but things were not the way they had imagined which was creating a lot of disappointment.

Armaan was a good man and did not ever want to hurt Arundhati, so he decided to reach out to a professional for some help. After understanding their history and background, the counsellor knew there was a lot of healing required for Arundhati and for Armaan to support her through this journey. They had to work extensively with Arundhati's past trauma through an integration of various counselling modalities which took over eighteen months. As a couple, they had highly frustrating days, exhausting days, and bad days, but through it all Armaan never lost hope and would be there for Arundhati with all his heart. It would be very frustrating for him as well but they both were able to move through the difficult time to come to a place where they were able to trust each other completely in all aspects.

For Arundhati, she did trust Armaan, but every time they would try to be intimate, her past memory would take her back to hearing her mother screaming for help from her bedroom. She had also seen the men in her family bring other women and she would remember her mother's crying face. Arundhati has seen her mother and other women in her family suffer greatly which was all etched in her and which had scarred her. This was what she needed to work through and understood that she also deserved a man who would respect her, take care of her and support her rather than hurt her. Deep down Arundhati felt she did not deserve this and would suffer like the other women in her family. It was not easy for Arundhati to even step into the counsellor's office as it was very difficult for her to trust anyone. In addition, there was immense shame she carried with her everywhere she went. It was only because of Armaan, she decided to give it a go. There were many pieces that Arundhati needed to work on, which she did with a lot of support from Armaan, which made it worthwhile. There were many pieces that came up for Armaan as well through therapy which he needed to work on which he did not shy away from. There was a deep sense of rejection that Armaan needed to work with which had roots in his childhood as well.

Physical intimacy is a very important part of being in love with someone, but their readiness is also highly crucial. Waiting for your partner to be ready builds more trust, security, safety, and reliability in any relationship. Taking things slow always helps to build stronger bonds. After many months of working on themselves and their relationship Armaan and Arundhati were in a better place where they were able to express their love to each other not only verbally but also physically.

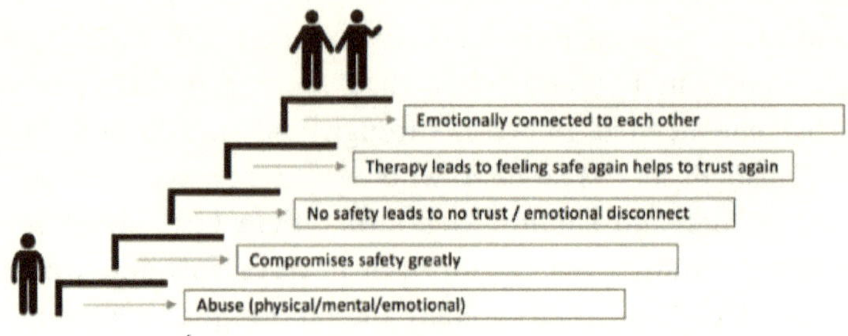

Illustration: Physical Intimacy

CHAPTER SEVEN

Respect

Very often it is said it is all about respecting others, but is it possible when one does not respect themselves?

Aahana and Ira, after fighting against the whole world, were finally together. They both never wanted to get married but wanted to live together. Firstly, they had to convince their families about their identity and preferences and then about living together without getting married. It was a long and difficult process. They both went through a lot of ups and downs after which finally the day came when they moved in together. The first two years were blissful for them both and it was more than they ever imagined. After two years things started shifting, once the comfort zone was established.

Ira started becoming overprotective about Aahana, which would suffocate Aahana and would lead her to distancing further from Ira. When the distance grew, it was not manageable for Ira so she would start over-extending herself in the relationship which was not who Ira was but had become due to the insecurity. This would lead Aahana to distance herself further and sometimes not show up in the relationship.

All of this would lead to them not communicating to each other for days. They would only argue and fight. Sometimes they did not understand what was going on and how their relationship had reached this stage. They both decided to reach out to a professional as it was getting from bad to worse and they were unable to figure a solution. Even if they tried, they would have few good days and then the old patterns would creep in, and it would ruin everything.

Ira came from a good family, but a family where her brothers were always a preference than her which had led her to feel not enough. She tried to prove herself and needed approval from the external world. Aahana came from a liberal family where she never had any restrictions so if anyone would get overprotective about her, it would question her freedom. For Aahana, when her freedom was restricted, it would make her feel she did not matter to the opposite person. When they would get tied up in their patterns it would prick on the trigger of "not feeling enough" for Ira and "*I* do not matter" for Aahana. This would lead them to play a dance between them of one pursuing and the other distancing or one would over-extend and the other would under-extend.

When these patterns are not addressed and healed, they create more distance in the relationship where one feels a deep sense of feeling stuck. Individuals start behaving in ways that are not a part of their original core self, and this is where one starts losing respect for self. We feel when we are stuck in these loops, we are losing respect for the other person as we are angry with them for not behaving the way we want them to behave or make us happy, but is this an appropriate ask?

Through the therapy sessions, both Ira and Aahana had to learn to understand who they are, their own patterns, and their own needs to begin with. They worked on letting go of parts of themselves that they did not resonate with and reclaiming parts of themselves that they resonated with. After which they were able to understand the opposite person so that they could show up in the relationship in the manner they needed to. They learnt to respect themselves and the space each one needed which brought them back to each other. They learnt to realign their expectations with each other keeping in mind the other person's capacity. They learnt not to over or under-extend in the relationship, as that was coming from a space of insecurity and the need to control the other person in some way. This was something they both worked on and replaced by understanding their needs and showing up in the relationship as required. They also learnt how to have conversations and hear each other rather than screaming and shouting at each other to be heard which never helped. They both really worked on themselves and their relationship which restored their faith back in each other to carry forward a beautiful relationship.

A relationship cannot only work on love, there are various other ingredients required to make it work like understanding, trust, faith, commitment, loyalty, and many more but one of the important ingredients is respect. It starts with respecting oneself which is equally important as respecting others.

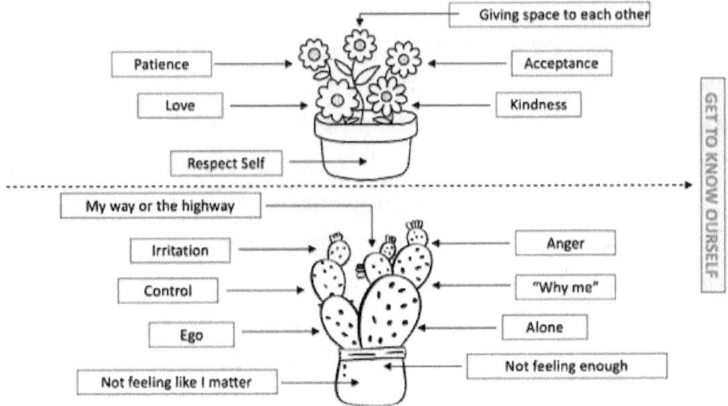

Illustration: Respect

Unhealthy Boundaries

Ankit had a very difficult childhood as his mother was verbally abusive, which never made him feel safe. Growing up he saw a lot of arguments and fights between his parents. He walked on eggshells pretty much his whole childhood. Ankit did not feel safe, so he never spoke about his feelings and emotions to anyone which affected his long-term relationship.

Aisha had a similar experience with her mother and was extremely afraid of her while growing up. Aisha had gone through a lot of physical abuse for no fault of hers. Her mother was not in the right frame of mind and was diagnosed with bipolar disorder, the brunt of which was borne by Aisha. Aisha never felt she mattered as she was yelled at and beaten for no reason. She never felt as though she was important for anyone.

As Ankit and Aisha came together, they brought forward their entire personality, the good and the not so good with them. Ankit had put up many walls in the relationship due to his unhealed past. He put up an unhealthy boundary where he would not speak about how he felt which caused more distance in the relationship. Aisha, due to her circumstances, brought her insecurity and inferiority complex in the relationship.

Aisha and Ankit were going through a boundary difficulty in their relationship which was unhealthy. They had put up high unhealthy boundaries due to their past trauma. As a couple, they were unable to understand, thereby making it difficult to regulate themselves. The relationship was smooth, but Ankit found it very challenging to open up to Aisha completely. They were together for more than five years, but there was an undercurrent of their past reflecting in the relationship. For Ankit, it would be very difficult to trust anyone so he would never have any relationship where he would talk about his own feelings or open up. For Aisha, it would always seem as though she did not matter/ was not important enough/not trustworthy. Whenever she would try to have deeper conversations, they both would end up talking more about Aisha, so her goodness and flaws were in the forefront and not Ankit's. It became a one-sided, Aisha focused conversation.

Through therapy, Aisha was able to understand and resolve her issues and gained a deeper understanding that it was not about her and that it was not her fault which made her realise her own value, worth and importance. On the other hand, Ankit's past was unhealed and was creating a divide between them. Through many sessions, Aisha was not dependent on Ankit to make her feel important which reduced the pressure from the relationship. For Ankit, working through his past helped him to understand the foundation of trust and start that process by first, trusting himself. He unlearned, changed, and moved towards building healthier habits. Ankit had to start with changing smaller habits step by step and through time when he was able to remain consistent with his new habits, it helped him to feel confident in himself and trust himself. This building of trust with self is what extended his trust in others as well over time. The more his trust grew in himself he was able to slowly open up to Aisha. It took them a long time, but they really stuck through the process with each other which helped them to heal from their own past wounds. It dawned on them that togetherness can have a profound impact on healing.

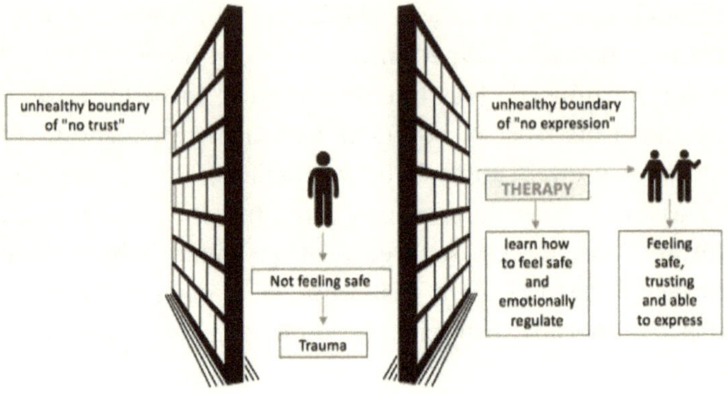

Illustration: Unhealthy Boundaries

CHAPTER NINE

Gaslighting

Mehru and Ali were childhood lovers. They had a smooth transition from dating to getting married as their families always knew they both would be together, and everyone was very happy about their union. They were very aware of each other's family background and upbringing. After five years of their marriage, things started shifting a bit. Somewhere they both started taking each other for granted and there came a time they did not feel as connected to each other. They would spend a lot of time without each other and on their own and in the company of their friends.

While growing up Mehru had seen her mother being a perfect individual. She would make sure to do everything right and being right was extremely important for her mother, and how to portray self in the society. Mehru looked up to her mother and always tried to emulate her. While for Ali, he was the elder brother and there was a lot of unrealized pressure on Ali to be a certain way and take on a lot of responsibility due to being the first born. He was not given the freedom to make any mistakes which over time moulded him into wanting to be the perfect person especially for his father. Many times, as children we tend to want to prove ourselves to our parents due to the expectations that have been laid out, which takes us away from being ourselves. Again, this is not to blame anyone, but the right kind of education needs to be shared with individuals to be able to function appropriately.

Mehru liked to stay busy all the time and would always fill up her plate because it was difficult for her to not be occupied. It is nice to have things to do but when an individual is trying to run away from certain feelings and choosing to stay busy all the time to avoid addressing what they are feeling, it speaks volumes. Though Mehru and Ali came from a similar upbringing they would look at a situation in two very different ways. Mehru was more emotional, and Ali would see it from a practical lens. There was no right or wrong but just accepting different ways of dealing with a similar situation was challenging for them. They would expect each other to do it in the manner each of them would approach it. This would always be a hindrance in their relationship which was unaddressed, but how long can things go unaddressed?

Over time this became a huge problem in their relationship as they both felt they were right in their own way and none of them would want to bend. They both were very strong individuals and being right was extremely important for them. Through time to prove their point they would gaslight each other in ways which was very hurtful for both. They would purposely say things to hurt and instigate each other as they both knew each other's sore points. They would purposely use words that triggered the other. They both started feeling suffocated in the relationship as they were constantly in conflict mode.

Mehru and Ali started distancing themselves and over time their relationship became a space of absolute bitterness. They had supportive family members who would try to help them, and momentarily, they would understand but then things would become sour again. The main cause of the problem was a pattern they both were dealing with which was unaddressed.

They both had to work through therapy to understand where this need to be right and perfect all the time even at the cost of their partner sprouted from. Being right was more important for them than who they would turn into in the process of proving themselves. They had become people they could not identify with. The need to be right was mollycoddling the ego which took them far away from who their core personality was. They both needed to work on taming their ego and swallowing their pride by learning it was okay not to be right and make mistakes and move away from the idea of perfectionism as nothing like that existed.

Gaslighting is an outcome of the fear of not wanting to be wrong. When a person does not want to own up to their doing, they tend to say things and do things in a way that the entire blame is shifted to the opposite person. For the time being, the focus shifts and the other person seems to be at fault. Then there is constant justification to continue to prove oneself right. Extremities can lead to lying, invalidating emotions, isolation, manipulations, etc.,

Many times, the need to be perfect, can take the shape of bitterness without one realising it. The need to be perfect individuals led them to the need of always wanting to be right and then in order to prove yourself as right, we can turn into individuals we are not. Gaslighting is one branch of the need to be right, which destroys relationships. Through working on letting go of the idea of perfectionism, Mehru and Ali, slowly and steadily, were in a better place with themselves, each other, and their relationship. They worked very hard on changing their perspective about the idea of perfectionism which reduced the need to be right all the time. They accepted that as individuals we need to love ourselves with the good and not-so-good parts of ourselves, as we are here to accept our whole self to learn and grow.

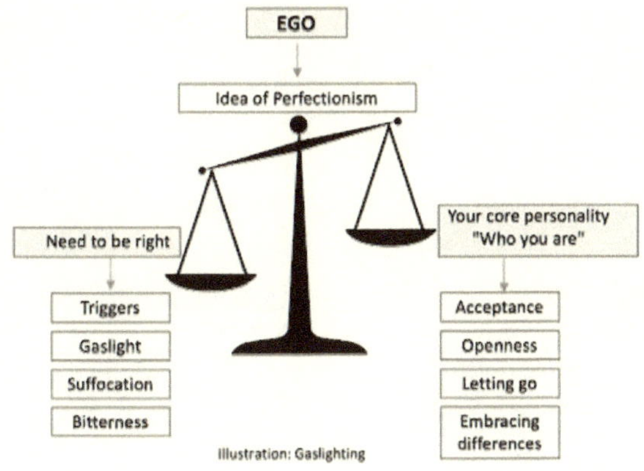

Illustration: Gaslighting

Words to Warm your Soul

CHAPTER TEN

Understanding

When two people come together, it is not only them who come together but an amalgamation of their dreams, aspirations, goals, characteristics, traits, values, principles, morals, hopes, and so much more. It is important to embrace this rather than the need to change any of this in the other person. But very often one tries to change the other person to fit into a mould that works for oneself, which is where all the problems begin. Love doesn't come with any conditions, therefore the more one keeps it unconditional the more one will be able to keep its essence alive. Love is about growing together not only from a materialistic aspect but also, a spiritual aspect.

With understanding comes a great deal of empathy. Without empathy, it becomes very difficult to understand the other person. Empathy cannot be felt for another person without feeling it for oneself. It starts with self. A quick way to check in with self is by checking the quality of one's self-dialogue. We all tend to talk to ourselves which is normal. Ask yourself, is my self-dialogue belittling or uplifting? This will shed some light on how empathetic you are towards yourself.

Another important aspect of any relationship is that many times one may not be the opposite person's priority, but one thinks that in an intimate relationship, they need to be the priority. Is this necessary? Isn't it okay to be second or third on the list of priorities? But when one is not strong in front of their ego and gives in to the ego, they then want to become the number one priority.

Couples that become better individuals in the process of love, respect each other. This foundation of trust and respect is imperative for any relationship to sustain and blossom. When one begins the journey towards love, having any other agenda besides love will not help in the long run. A true companion will always help the other person to be the way they are and help to always come back to their original essence, if they stray, which is where being a patient, understanding partner becomes a saving grace for the relationship.

When one can understand each relationship, starting with yourself, it becomes easy to extend support and space for other relationships too. Most individuals feel misunderstood or not understood in their relationship which leads to feeling unsupported as well. For understanding to remain in any relationship the most important aspect is communication. There is this expectation from the partner to magically understand everything one wants, and desires, but pausing for a moment to introspect, one asks, is it possible? Yes, there may be times the partner will understand but most times they will not, and not because they don't want to understand but because we are also constantly changing.

When one does not keep up to their own self-changes, how will another person keep up with it? Remember unrealistic expectations make an individual less understanding, more rigid and stubborn.

Many times, therapists are asked questions of how an individual can become more empathetic. From a personal point of view, being empathetic is deeply related to healing. The more empathetic one becomes; the more healing happens from within. Empathy is about being soft and gentle with self, at every stage of life. One can be empathetic towards self which is by itself a very difficult process because very often one is self-judgemental. Being understanding and empathetic is very crucial for two people to come together and feel safe and secure in their togetherness and opens the door to being authentic in any relationship.

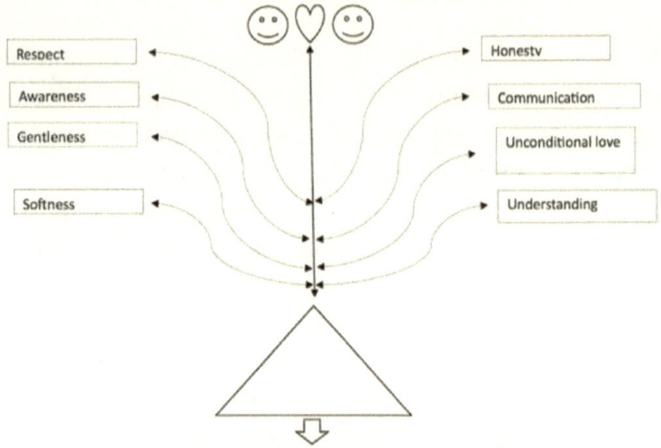

Understanding and Empathy Towards Self and Others

Illustration: Understanding

CHAPTER ELEVEN

Communication

How is it so difficult to communicate what is going on internally inside a person? Have you ever given it a thought? There is a huge piece where individuals feel very judged, therefore they prefer not speaking up about what they are feeling as it may change how the opposite person will view them. They have set up the environment so that others think of them in a certain way and if they speak up, they may not be as liked. But isn't this more about individuals judging themselves rather than others judging them? Fear of judgement comes from a place of insecurities like not feeling adequate, so if this is something that is coming up for you then please take some time to work through it.

When one thinks of intimate relationships, there is an expectation from the partner that they need to understand me, without me having to say anything. Yes, that would be ideal but is that realistic? No human is a magician, and will understand exactly what you desire or would like in the moment. Yes, there may be times one understands but it may not happen every time. Communication is the soul of every relationship. It can sometimes be hard, but it is necessary to speak your mind. When we communicate our needs with our partner it brings two people closer and reduces the potential of misunderstandings. It helps to have clarity and to get to know each other better.

It is communication that bridges the gap between two individuals. Many times, couples refrain from communicating which is a huge drawback as it prolongs the pain. Especially when there is a fight or an argument, many couples tend to stop speaking to each other for days. Yes, many people need their time to come back to stability after any conflict but once you do feel more balanced, complete the conversation rather than letting it slide. When these conversations are not addressed, it has the potential to resurface later with compound interest.

Communication is one of the best tools to have in your pocket in life. It can save individuals from a lot of disappointment. Assumptions will not help but communication will surely help, so do not step back from speaking your mind. Communication and respect go hand in hand so please don't use one without the other. Communication is another form of verbal expression, which is extremely important for individuals to empty themselves, so do not escape this beautiful process, embrace it.

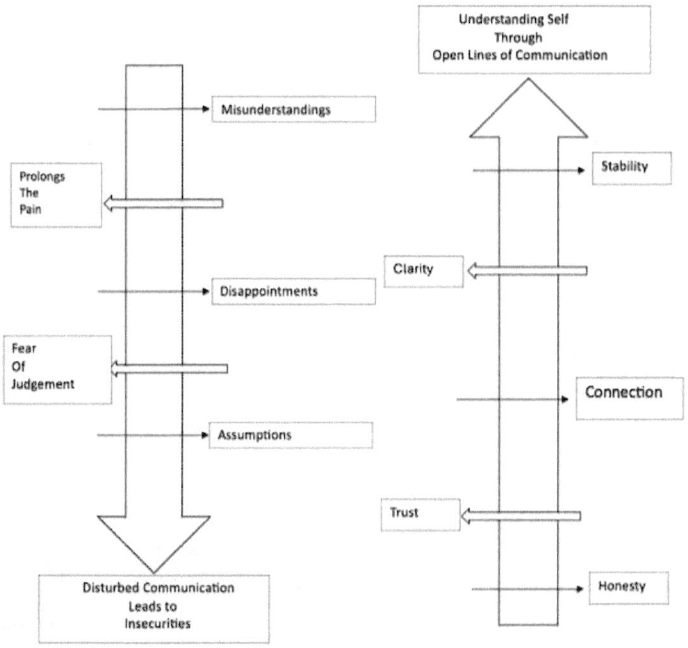

Illustration: Communication

CHAPTER TWELVE

Self-Reliance

We live in a society that has conditioned us to believe that, individually, we are not complete. It is our partner that completes us. Is this true? The answer to this question is a BIG NO. Yes, we need each other, and we need to learn to coexist, but nobody completes anybody. The first expectation that needs to be reworked in any relationship is that my partner completes me so he/she/they will keep me happy forever. This thought process is the downfall for many relationships. Nobody can be responsible for keeping someone happy, it is solely your responsibility to keep yourself happy. Each individual needs to fill their own cup of happiness. When we become highly dependent on others to make us feel good about ourselves, even if they want to, they will not be able to serve us as it is humanly not possible to do that. Yes, occasionally someone may be able to do this for you, which is a gift for you. But having that expectation all the time is when you are doing a disservice to yourself. As the message you are sending to yourself is, you are not capable of keeping yourself happy, which is not true.

Let's look at this in a percentage form, it is okay to expect someone to keep you happy 15% of the time but 85% of the time it is your own responsibility to keep yourself happy. When the percentage is reversed, is where all the problems begin. You can also think of it as every month's salary is something you need to work hard for which helps you to be happy when you see that paycheck in your bank account. Occasionally, you will see the bonus in your bank account, which does not come in every month. So would you expect a bonus to come in every month just because it makes you happy, no, you will be happy with your salary. In the same manner, you need to fill your own cup, if someone comes and adds something to your cup it is great, just like the bonus, but your filled cup from your end is what you are relying on which is your salary.

In an intimate relationship, this is extremely important to execute or else it becomes an imbalance relationship which is very hard to sustain in the long run. Learn to take the reins of happiness back into your own hands.

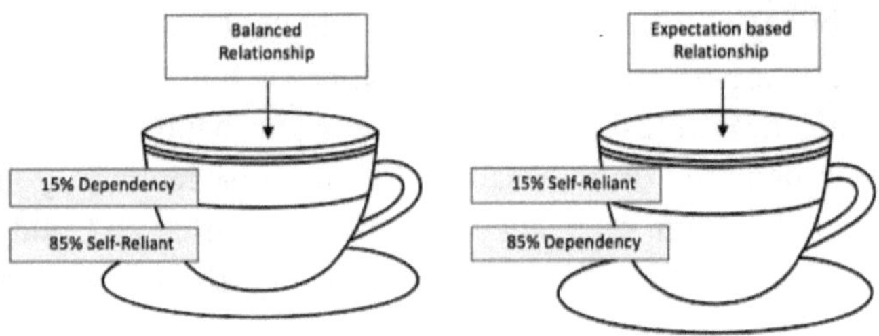

Illustration: Self Reliance

CHAPTER THIRTEEN

Kindness and Forgiveness

There are plenty of ways to be kind and we all are aware of those. When we look at relationships, kindness can be shown by practising forgiveness. Every relationship goes through many ups and downs and the only way to move forward from painful experiences is by showing kindness in the form of forgiving yourself and letting go of the toxic feelings gathered for another. There are many difficult moments one goes through in any relationship but when we can look at it as a learning ground, it is possible to move in the direction of forgiveness. Please note, that we are not asking anyone to be in any abusive or toxic environment.

Forgiveness does not only apply to present relationships but also to those that have not worked out. To move forward from broken relationships, one must be kind to oneself which will enable you to walk on the path of forgiveness. Healing takes place when we are kind to all ages and phases of our life. When we learn to practice this by going inward and searching for that kindness, we open the door to learning what forgiveness means and how to go about it.

In one of the books, called "The Seat of the Soul" by Gary Zukav, very beautifully he explained how it is important for everyone to look at another person, just as a human being without any titles of mother, father, spouse, sister, brother, etc., as it is then we can let go of expectations that sprout from these various titles and understand we are all here to learn and work on ourselves. This understanding makes one realise the extreme need for kindness we all are in dire need of which takes us towards letting go and forgiveness. This perspective is very important for us to grow as human beings and to become more awakened spiritually.

Yes, we all feel the pain and immense hurt, but please know we can all rise above that if we practice kindness. Start with being kind to self, by not speaking in a demeaning manner to self, by not judging self, by extending an understanding to self which we usually extend to others. When we slowly start liking ourselves more and more, we understand carrying any past or present burdens is not in sync with your true essence which invokes the need to walk on the path of forgiveness. Forgiveness is a portal to freedom which we are all in search of.

When two people come together, they are essentially there to help and lift each other. With each other's support this journey becomes more worthwhile, so change the lens towards your relationships and see the shift in yourself and slowly in people around you. There is a give and take in every relationship and when we stop fighting that, things don't seem to hurt as much.

Being gentle and kind comes when we go inward and understand we all are evolving through time and with experiences. We all have done things that do not align with who we are due to various factors, but it is important to be able to go internally and understand every moment of our life, we are at a different stage of evolution, so our behaviour reflects that stage. Yes, sometimes it may be very hard to see in the mirror but, we must keep working in that direction, to keep showing ourselves that kindness, till one day with your strong desire, we can show kindness to ourselves through walking on the journey of forgiveness. This is an important universal lesson for each individual as we are all here to learn. When we learn to be kind to ourselves, it becomes an extension of who we are which carries forward outside of ourselves as well. For any relationship to sustain, kindness as a virtue is extremely important as it helps you to gain an understanding of another through the lens of innocence. Many times, we lose this innocence due to the pain and hurt we are feeling, but it is kindness that keeps this innocence alive in us which then will lead us to the path of forgiveness which we all need to live a free life.

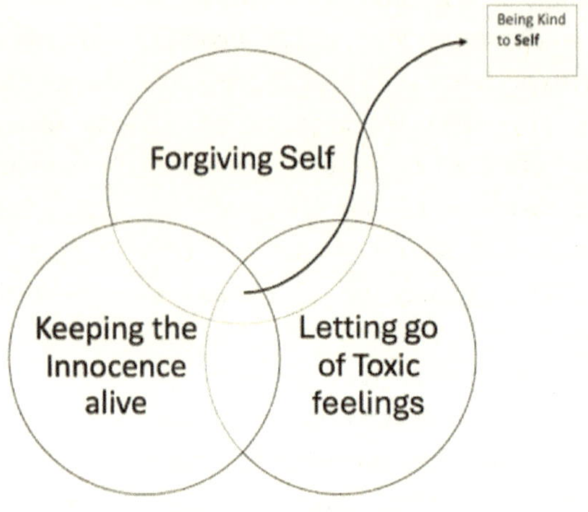

Illustration: Kindness and Forgiveness

CHAPTER FOURTEEN

Healthy Boundaries

Do boundaries have space in a relationship? Or should there be no boundaries in a relationship? Take some time to ponder over these questions and see what comes up for you.

Please know boundaries are a healthy aspect of every relationship whether it is an intimate relationship or not. Boundaries help individuals to feel safe when respected and adhered to. Safety is one of the most important feelings in any relationship, especially in an intimate relationship. Without safety, it becomes quite challenging for any individual to be their true self in any equation or situation.

Boundaries are what gives an insight into a person so one can understand themselves deeply. Boundaries usually reflect one's past experiences. Based on those, every individual creates certain boundaries that cannot and should not be crossed. It is extremely important to communicate personal boundaries, so the opposite person is aware. Please note boundaries can change over time so one-time communication does not suffice. As one matures and grows, boundaries will expand and change.

Boundary violation is a path to breaking trust. This is something from which one should try and stay miles away as it scars a soul and takes a lifetime to rebuild. Boundary violation speaks more about the person who violated the boundary than the person who created them. Ridiculing a boundary can lead to creating a lot of disturbance in any relationship. If one does not agree that may be alright, but agreeing to disagree is the way to go ahead. An individual can give suggestions or opinions when asked but one should learn to respect the boundary created.

Boundaries are important, as in the past when they have been ambushed, it has hurt the person, and the individual is trying to protect themselves. Therefore, understanding this is very vital to bring in the aspect of safety, trust, and respect in any relationship.

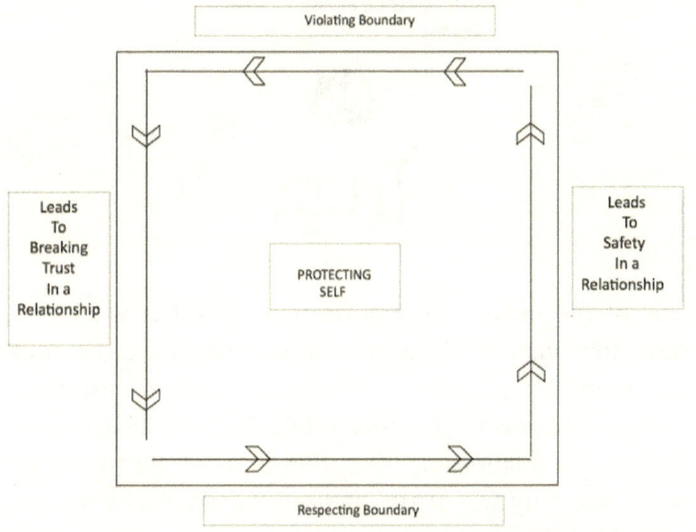

Illustration: Healthy Boundaries

CHAPTER FIFTEEN

Trust

One of the innate expectations everyone has when they start any relationship is this person will have my back. The more you see that in your partner, your trust grows in the relationship. Do you think this will sustain your trust in the relationship? Yes, this is important to feel but is this the only way trust can keep growing? The reason I ask this question is so one can reflect and understand as much as this is required, this is where we are still relying on an external source. Where are we doing our work to increase trust?

Getting assurance from your partner is a lovely feeling, but again that is 15%. What about our own 85%? Please understand trust is something we need to work internally to build within ourselves. Trust begins first with YOU. For which we need to understand that "I will have my own back no matter what". We often rely on others to show up for us and there is nothing wrong in that in a reasonable manner, but we must show up for ourselves as well. It is this that builds the trust within yourself which is what we are constantly looking for in others.

Trusting self means building an authentic relationship with self, where you can rely on yourself. This reliability comes only when daily you show up for yourself. For example, when you tell yourself you will be at a particular place or wake up at a particular time, you show up for yourself. It is about starting with the very small things and slowly you will see your ability building which will help you to expand your trust in yourself. This will slowly lead to you learning to trust your decisions whether it is on a personal or professional front.

The more you continue to implement this, you will have a stronger relationship with yourself making you more confident in your ability to make choices and decisions. This is how we start working and learning how to trust ourselves. It is a step-by-step process so please keep patience as your closest best friend on this journey towards building trust. In any relationship when we keep up to a promise the trust grows, which is extremely crucial for two people to feel the trust between them. In the same manner, we need to learn to keep up to our own promises towards ourselves, as that is what will keep expanding the trust and lead to being your authentic self.

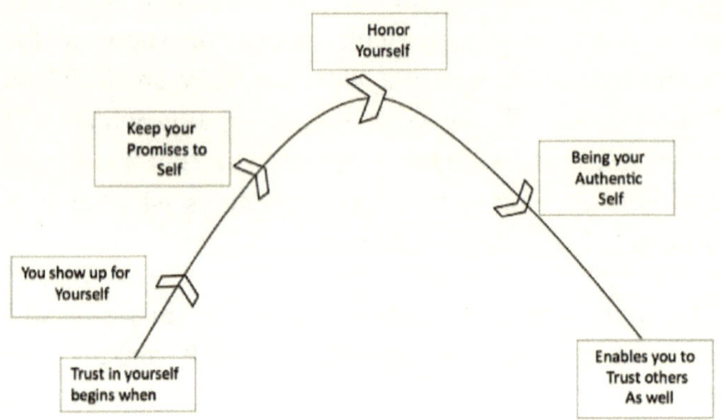

Illustration: Trust

CHAPTER SIXTEEN

Unconditional Connection

Togetherness is vital for co-existence, but we need to widen our horizons to understand what togetherness truly means. It has a deeper meaning than just the surface-level understanding. It is not about this person who will take care of me, my needs and my family. Togetherness is all about unconditional connection that is built between two people who have come together in this life to help each other grow spiritually and become better human beings. When this remains the focus in relationships, they last as they have a purpose together but when it becomes all about the surface level things, the relationship is more temporary by nature.

It is time we understand the meaning of unconditional connection. When two people step into a lifelong bond, it is at that moment they have agreed to serve each other in their profound spiritual journey. We all need each other to walk through this path, it is where we invite ourselves and our partner to be their true self and accept them just as is without the need to change them in any way, shape, or form. This is where we are in flow with what is meant to be and understand the higher meaning and purpose of being with someone.

In the times we live, we are slowly losing the true essence of being with another person. A partnership is beyond any materialistic temptation, it is not about status, it is not only about "me" but "how can we help each other to grow spiritually". It is about how we can become better individuals and how we can be more fulfilled by supporting and being there for each other. It is about dedication, loyalty, and commitment to spiritual growth.

The path to spiritual growth in Relationships

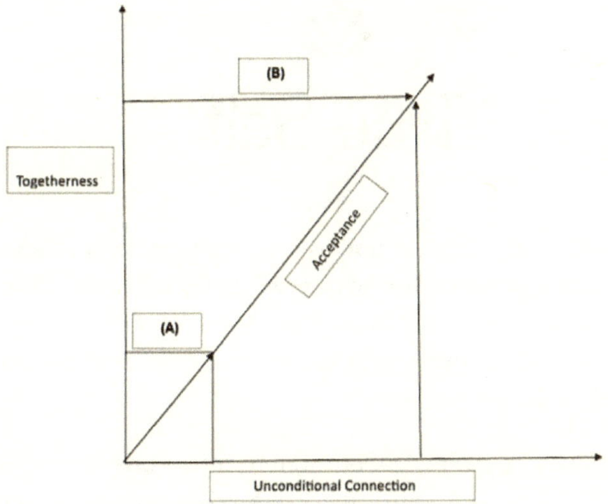

The choice is whether one wants option (A) or (B)

Illustration: Unconditional Connection

CHAPTER SEVENTEEN

True Self

We need to take time to understand who we are and what is our life's purpose for which we need to come closer to our creator and stay away from temptation and greed. When we are in touch with our creator, that is when our true self will surface.

We need to work on our inner intentions and keep cleaning them and purifying them. The more we feel connected to the divine, the more we are on the path of truth and honesty. In this world, it is not easy to be your true self, therefore without the help and strength from the creator, it becomes very difficult to continue to grow spiritually. Therefore, take every moment you can to connect with your creator.

We all have two sides in us - one is the things we need to improve on, and the other is the innate goodness we all have due to the various experiences we have been through. Each one of us has a choice which side to activate. The side that is more activated becomes more familiar to us. Paying attention to any one side will not lead us to a balanced lifestyle. The recipe to a peaceful life is to stay in the middle and become balanced individuals. When we continue to introspect this, we slowly get answers about who we are and what is our true nature. When this is done in unison with a higher understanding, it helps to go beyond the physical existence of an individual, into the realm of your soul and what you have come here to do. With time, this search will take you to the depths of your true self. You will be able to align yourself to the essence of your true self, to lead life in a very fulfilling manner. This is where all fear is lost as fear is then replaced by immense faith. Where there is faith, there are no hindrances. This is where your faith in your creator knows no bounds, and you can feel the essence of your creator.

This journey is possible, but as a human, we need to create the urge and thirst to want to experience it. It is a journey that takes you inward to then truly learn the art of detachment which reduces your expectations from others around you, leading you to a deeper sense of acceptance of self and others around you.

It is in silence, that you can go inward and understand the essence of your true self. The more you can embody it and connect to it, you will experience an absolute state of bliss. This leads to having a very different perspective of life which keeps you away from getting entangled. This understanding does not allow you to get caught in anything and even if you do, it becomes easier to step off the entangled situation with your understanding of life.

So, take time to go on this beautiful journey with yourself, and learn the universal lesson of detachment, letting go and acceptance which are very essential to maintain relationships in a healthy manner.

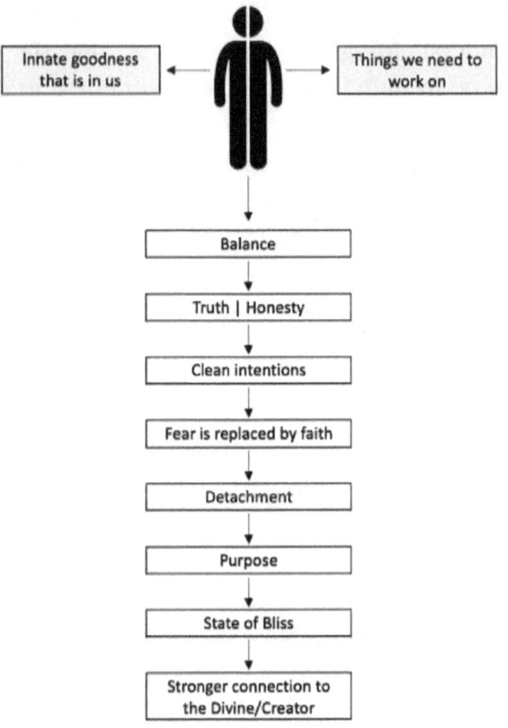

Illustration: True Self

CHAPTER EIGHTEEN

Transformation Through Action

As logical human beings, we doubt this absolute reality. We dodge it from time to time. But the fact of life remains- "what we sow, we reap". One can see it in every aspect of nature. Therefore, we need to lead a life in unison with this concept. Life gets a wee bit easier if not a whole lot. But isn't that what we are seeking for all the time?

When we plant a seed, we get flowers and when one plants a bomb, we get destruction. Now from a human perspective, how does this work? Your answer sits in the intention. Therefore, it is imperative what we say, think and feel need to be in alignment. A slight shift in your intention will reflect in your thoughts, feelings, which leads to the action. Your action at the end of the day is very powerful. But our job is to work with the intention as then the action will be an automatic flow.

In relationships, everything is transparent. Nothing can be hidden, therefore it is very important to be honest, as the opposite person can sense it. We all can sense things whether we accept it or not. Therefore, manipulation never works, no matter how much a person tries to hide things, eventually the truth will prevail. As mentioned earlier, your intention is the most important as it eventually drives your actions. So, work on purifying your intentions.

We all are here to learn and grow, learn lessons that will help us to become better individuals. Some need to learn resistance, some need to learn how to be flexible, some need to learn how to be happy with less, some need to learn to be selfless, and so forth. The more we understand ourselves, we can understand what we are here to learn through all the different experiences we are attracting. If you take time to sit and understand, you will notice there must be a sequence or a particular similarity in all your experiences as we are here to learn something that is unique to your soul.

Similarly, we attract partners from whom we need to learn and vice-versa. Keeping this in mind will reduce the arguments and conflicts between two individuals as now you are seeing this relationship from a higher frequency lens.

Take time to reflect on how you found this one person to be together with, amongst so many people on this planet, of course, there must be something that connected both of you towards each other. Imagine how beautiful that thought is. But when we come together instead of cherishing each other and accepting each other, we start trying to change the essence of each other. Do you think this is fair? Are we here to change another or ourselves?

Please take some time to ponder over this question.

When there is a strong union of two individuals, they can learn from each other and not feel inferior or superior in any way. Togetherness can make your path a bit lighter and there is a beautiful sense of companionship.

We all have our dues to pay whether we like it or not or accept it or not. But with some support, it keeps us from becoming bitter. Every reaction or action is equivalent to a reaction or action. Therefore, please be aware of what you will take from others, you will need to give it back in some way, as this is the law of nature. Despite the growth and development of the modern world of science, we cannot change any laws that come from the divine.

When two people come together they bring a lot into the relationship, which is a natural process, so instead of staying in a conflict mode, embrace, accept and flow with each other. With this mindset, both individuals can help to set each other free from the burdens they have been carrying for so long from their past or/and present. When we adopt this perspective in a relationship, we will create more space in the relationship to accept each other the way they are instead of trying to change one another so desperately. Please know that nobody changes till they feel the need to.

Your actions create your life, so focus on your intention that constantly backs up your action. The more you can align your thoughts, feelings, and actions, the more in sync you will feel within yourself and with others around you. You will not need to work on changing others but yourself.

• 78 •

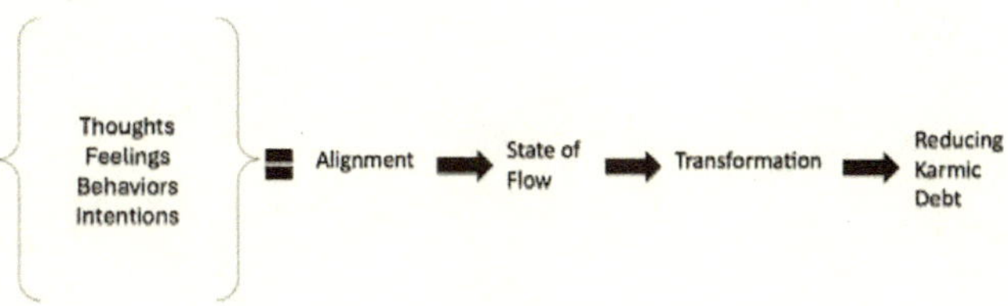

Illustration: Transformation through Action

Conclusion

Patience is a quality you will need throughout this book, as feelings that you may have never felt may come up or a different perspective may arise which you may like or not like. But be assured it would be something that would be beneficial towards your growth as a human being. So, keep patience as your closest friend throughout this journey. Some topics may have a deeper connection with you than others, and the more you put them into practice, the more will be revealed to you. We have lived with these beliefs for many years so give yourself some time and a fair chance to move through it. Truly hope you can practice this book in your daily life which will not only help you but also the people around you. This will bring an authentic change in your life, one that will make you walk on the path of freedom, something we all long for. Give your best and that is what you will get in return. Would like to conclude with a quote that has greatly impacted my life.

"Do the best you can until you know better. Then when you know better, do better."
— Maya Angelou

About The Author

I come from India, a land of colour, food, variety, spirituality, warmth, culture and much more. I grew up in Mumbai in a loving, kind and giving family. After spending 23 years of my life in Mumbai, I moved to Vancouver. My first 5 years in Vancouver were a struggle, as I had to adapt to a significantly different culture and societal norms. I come from a family of diamond merchants, and I am a Jewellery Designer and a Diamond Grader. I will always try and cultivate my family diamond jewellery business and have been a Human Resources

Professional in the corporate world for several years. Clay Consulting, is my practice wherein I am a Life Coach, Master Coach, Registered Holistic Nutritionist and a Registered Therapeutic Counsellor. After spending almost 12 years in Vancouver, I am back in Mumbai, attending to clients from all walks of life. In my spare time I love to dance, as I am a professionally trained dancer, and I enjoy singing as well.

This book will give you insight not only on working on yourself but in relation to another as well which is extremely important as that is where you get to practice all what you have learnt through time and experiences. Take time to ponder over what resonates with you and to internalise your learnings which can reflect in your behaviour and actions moving forward. One of the things I have learnt, we are waiting for the change to occur in the opposite person, and this is where it is not in our control, so let's change this and focus on what is in our control which is to bring the change in yourself. This is something we owe to ourselves so don't worry about anything else but SHOW UP FOR YOURSELF and MAKE THE NECESSARY CHANGE.

Thank you

* 9 7 9 8 8 8 9 5 5 6 2 2 0 8 *